My First Book of Nature

Birds

Victoria Munson

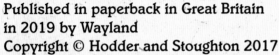

Published in paperback in Great Britain in 2019 by Wayland
Copyright © Hodder and Stoughton 2017

Wayland
Carmelite House
50 Victoria Embankment
London
EC4Y 0DZ

Editor: Victoria Brooker
Designer: Elaine Wilkinson

A cataloguing record for this title is available at the British Library.

ISBN: 978 1 5263 0121 5

Printed in China

MIX
Paper from responsible sources
FSC® C104740
www.fsc.org

Wayland, part of Hachette Children's Group and published by Hodder and Stoughton Limited.
www.hachette.co.uk

Acknowledgements:
All graphics Shutterstock.com, and cover: main Mark Medcalf tr Menno Schaefer; tl Alexander Erdbeer; bl Jozef Sowa; br Cric Isselee; 1, 6 Edwin/Butter/; 4 Dominique de La Croix; 5t ChameleonsEye; 5b dmodlin01; 6b Howard Marsh; 7t Karel Gallas; 7b Martin Fowler; 8l Marc Goldman; 8r John Navajo; 9t Bildagentur Zoonar GmbH; 9b Visayas; 10l Zakharov Aleksey; 10r Erni; 11 Rudmer Zwerver; 12 Belen Bilgic Schneider; 13t Arvind Balaraman; 13b Juan Roballo; 14t MAC1; 14b Paul Cummings; 15t V. Belov; 16 Rafal Szozda; 17t Mark Medcalf; 17b Tobyphotos; 18 Jack53; 19 Michal Ninger; 20 Rafal Szozda; 21t Bildagentur Zoonar GmbH; 21b Drakuliren; 11, 19t istock by Getty Images

Every attempt has been made to clear copyright. Should there be an inadvertent omission, please apply to the Publisher for rectification.

Contents

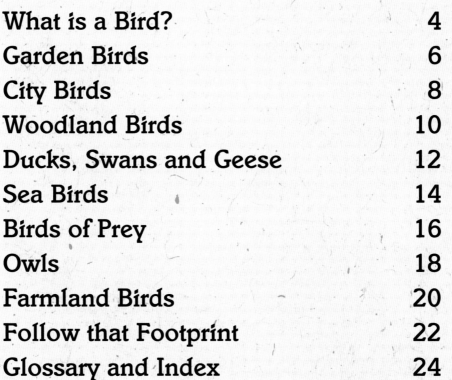

What is a Bird?

Birds are warm-blooded animals that can lay eggs. A bird has feathers and wings. No other animal has feathers. Birds have a beak but no teeth.

Feathers are used to keep birds warm,

help them to fly and provide camouflage.

Most birds can fly. However, there are some birds that don't. These include penguins, ostriches and kiwis.

Penguins are very strong swimmers and ostriches are fast runners.

Ostriches can run at 97 kph.

Penguins live at the cold South Pole.

Birds are found all over the world. Parrots are found in hot rainforests.

Flamingoes live together in large groups near lakes and swamps.

Garden Birds

Robins are small birds with bright red breasts. They love to sing, from early morning to late at night.

Robins eat apples, nuts and even spiders.

Male blackbirds have a bright yellowish-orange beak.

Blackbirds eat worms, berries and fruit.

Blue tits are good at hanging upside down from bird feeders. Their bright blue head and wings with a yellow breast makes them easy to recognise.

Great tits have a black line down the middle of their yellow breasts. They have a glossy black head with white cheeks.

teacher teacher

Listen out for great tits' 'teacher teacher' call.

Great tits love peanuts, fat balls, seeds and insects.

City Birds

Male House Sparrows have a black head and neck with white cheeks. Female sparrows are brown with no black markings.

Sparrows are very common in towns and cities.

Magpies are large, black **and white birds.**

Magpie nests sometimes have roofs and two entrances. Listen for their loud chattering call.

chatter

chatter

Starlings live together in large flocks. A group of starlings is called a chattering.

Pigeons are the most common city bird. They are grey with shades of green and purple on their neck.

Starlings are very good at copying the sound of other birds, mammals or even telephones!

Ring! Ring!

Pigeons live in large groups to protect themselves from predators such as cats, foxes and rats.

Woodland Birds

Song thrushes have heart-shaped brown spots on their cream-coloured breasts. Mistle thrushes look very similar but are slightly larger.

Jays are brightly coloured, large birds, with pinkish-brown bodies and blue and black wings.

Look for jays in autumn when they come down from the trees to bury acorns.

Great spotted woodpeckers are black and white with a red patch under their tail.

Woodpeckers have two toes facing forward and two facing backwards.

Nuthatches are small colourful birds with blue-grey wings and orange-brown breasts.

Nuthatches have a thick black line over each eye. Look for them walking upside down on hazel and beech trees.

Ducks, Swans and Geese

Mallards are the most common type of duck in Britain. Male mallards have a green head, yellow beak and white ring around their neck. Female mallards are speckled brown.

Don't feed ducks bread. It is bad for them. Instead feed them seeds and berries.

Swans are very large white birds.

Swans have a long s-shaped neck. When angry, they will hiss and flap their wings.

Young swans are called cygnets.

Canada geese have long black necks and white cheeks. Large flocks of geese group together in parks and fields.

Look up to see these geese flying by in a 'v' shape.

Canada geese can fly at 30 mph.

Moorhens are black with a red forehead. They live in ponds, rivers and lakes. Their long green toes help them to grip on wet stones.

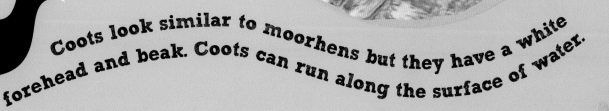

Coots look similar to moorhens but they have a white forehead and beak. Coots can run along the surface of water.

Sea Birds

Herring gulls are large, noisy birds. They have a red spot on their curved yellow beaks. When hungry chicks peck the red spot on the adult's beak, the adult knows to open it and give food to their young.

In summer, black-headed gulls have black heads. For the rest of the year, their head has brown stripes. They like to live in groups.

As well as fish, gulls also eat worms and insects.

Oystercatchers have black and white bodies with long, bright orange beaks. They use their long beaks to open mussel shells.

Puffins live in groups on cliffs. They are black and white with a very colourful curved beak and bright orange legs.

Puffins eat tiny silver fish called sand eels.

Birds of Prey

Red kites are a reddish-brown colour with white patches under their wings.

They have a huge wingspan of nearly **2 metres.**

Red kites have long, sharp talons for grabbing their prey.

Look for red kites sat on top of telegraph posts near roadsides.

Sparrowhawks have a bar pattern across their chest. They do not hover like kestrels, but fly quickly looking for small birds to eat.

The sparrowhawk's hooked beak helps it to scoop up prey.

Kestrels are small birds of prey with a long tail and pointed wings.

Kestrels eat small mammals such as mice and voles.

They hover above the ground before swooping down on their prey.

Owls

Barn owls have a snowy white breast and honey-coloured back and wings. Their white face is heart-shaped.

Owls are usually nocturnal, which means they hunt at night, but barn owls can sometimes be seen in the daytime.

Look for barn owls in the early evening perched by a roadside. They are waiting to swoop down and catch mice and voles.

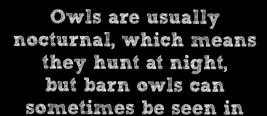

Long-eared owls are light brown with dark brown streaks. They get their name from their long ears! They have a dark-brown, round face with orange eyes.

Males have loud hoots that can be heard up to 1 km away. **Hooot!**

Short-eared owls have a brownish-black body, white face and yellow eyes. Owls swallow their prey whole.

Short-eared owls can be seen hunting in the daytime.

Farmland Birds

Pheasants have beautiful long tail feathers. Males are dark golden brown with a green head and red face wattles.

Females are paler brown and black. Look for them at field edges.

Pheasants have excellent sight and hearing, which they use to help them avoid predators, such as foxes and birds of prey.

Redwings look like thrushes but have a bright red patch under their wings and a yellow stripe above their eyes.

In autumn, you can see flocks of hundreds of redwings.

Grey partridges have an orange face and mottled grey feathers. Their wings make a loud whirring noise when they fly.

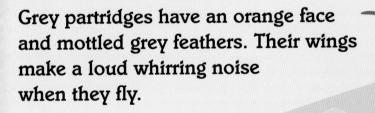

Grey partridges lay one of the largest clutches of eggs in the world – 15 to 19 per nest.

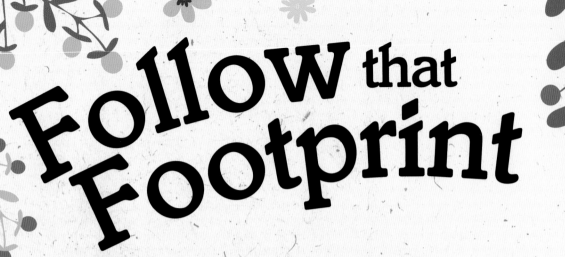

Follow that Footprint

Sometimes it's hard to spot animals. Find out if a bird has been nearby by looking for clues.

Duck

In soft mud, birds will leave footprints behind.

Crow

Look at the footprints and see if you can spot any in your local wildlife habitat.

Moorhen

Bird of prey

Glossary and Index

camouflage colours on an animal's body that blend with the background, making it difficult to spot

predator an animal that hunts, kills and eats other animals

prey an animal that is hunted and killed for food for another animal

warm-blooded having a body temperature that remains steady and warm, no matter what the outside temperature is. Mammals and birds are warm-blooded animals.